AUGUST

A new era for Arsenal Football Club kicked off on Sunday, August 12, 2018. Unai Emery's first game in charge of the Gunners was at home against defending Premier League champions Manchester City. New signings Sokratis, Matteo Guendouzi, Stephan Lichtsteiner and Lucas Torreira all made their debuts but despite some encouraging signs, we fell to an opening-day defeat. Henrikh Mkhitaryan scored our first goal of the season in our next game, at Stamford Bridge. We fought back from 2-0 down to level before half-time, but again went home empty-handed after a late goal from the hosts.

The following week we were off and running, showing great resolve to beat West Ham at home after again conceding first. Nacho Monreal's equaliser was a particular highlight – coming at the end of a 16-pass move.

RESULTS

Sun 12	Premier League	Manchester City (H)	0-2
Sat 18	Premier League	Chelsea (A)	2-3
		Mkhitaryan, Iwobi	
Sat 25	Premier League	West Ham United (H)	3-1
		Monreal, Diop (og), Welbeck	

↗ Arsenal.com Player of the Month
Matteo Guendouzi

7

SEPTEMBER

The winning form continued into September – we won all six matches in three different competitions, scoring 16 goals in the process.

We edged a five-goal thriller at Cardiff, with Pierre-Emerick Aubameyang and Alexandre Lacazette scoring their first goals of the season. We won again on the road after the international break, beating Newcastle, before our Europa League campaign got underway with a win over Ukrainian side Vorskla Poltava.

Our first clean sheet followed in the 2-0 win over Everton, and we progressed in the Carabao Cup, knocking out Brentford thanks to a brace from Danny Welbeck. Two late goals in the final game of the month against Watford gave us another three points and lifted us to fifth place.

RESULTS

Sun 2	Premier League	**Cardiff City** (A) *Mustafi, Aubameyang, Lacazette*	**3-2**
Sat 15	Premier League	**Newcastle United** (A) *Xhaka, Ozil*	**2-1**
Thur 20	Europa League	**Vorskla Poltava** (H) *Aubameyang 2, Welbeck, Ozil*	**4-2**
Sun 23	Premier League	**Everton** (H) *Lacazette, Aubameyang*	**2-0**
Wed 26	Carabao Cup	**Brentford** (H) *Welbeck 2, Lacazette*	**3-1**
Sat 29	Premier League	**Watford** (H) *Cathcart (og), Ozil*	**2-0**

➔ Arsenal.com Player of the Month
Alexandre Lacazette

Three players – Sokratis, Emile Smith Rowe and Guendouzi – all claimed their first goals for the club in a convincing Europa League group stage win in Baku, Azerbaijan – where we would return for the final in May.

The wins kept coming in the Premier League too. Fulham were dispatched 5-1 at Craven Cottage with Aaron Ramsey scoring one of the goals of the season, finishing an incredible, fast-passing move with a cheeky backheel. There was another mesmeric goal in the next win over Leicester City – this time Aubameyang put the finishing touch to some exquisite build-up play involving Ozil and Lacazette. It would pip Ramsey's effort to be voted Arsenal's Goal of the Season.

Three days later we made it 11 wins on the spin, thanks to Welbeck's strike away to Sporting Lisbon. We dropped points for the first time since August in a 2-2 draw at Crystal Palace, but responded to knock Blackpool out of the Carabao Cup – Lichtsteiner bagging his first goal for the club.

Striker Aubameyang had netted five league goals in October, enough to earn him the Premier League Player of the Month award.

RESULTS

Thur 4	Europa League	**Qarabag** (A) *Sokratis, Smith Rowe, Guendouzi*	**3-0**
Sun 7	Premier League	**Fulham** (A) *Lacazette 2, Ramsey, Aubameyang 2*	**5-1**
Mon 22	Premier League	**Leicester City** (H) *Ozil, Aubameyang 2*	**3-1**
Thur 25	Europa League	**Sporting Lisbon** (A) *Welbeck*	**1-0**
Sun 28	Premier League	**Crystal Palace** (A) *Xhaka, Aubameyang*	**2-2**
Wed 31	Carabao Cup	**Blackpool** (H) *Lichtsteiner, Smith Rowe*	**2-1**

↗ **Arsenal.com Player of the Month**
Pierre-Emerick Aubameyang

RESULTS			
Sat 3	Premier League	Liverpool (H)	1-1
		Lacazette	
Thur 8	Europa League	Sporting Lisbon (H)	0-0
Sun 11	Premier League	Wolves (H)	1-1
		Mkhitaryan	
Sun 25	Premier League	Bournemouth (A)	2-1
		Lerma (og), Aubameyang	
Thur 29	Europa League	Vorskla Poltava (A)	3-0
		Smith Rowe, Ramsey, Willock	

NOVEMBER

We extended our unbeaten run to 13 games with a draw against table-topping Liverpool which kept us within four points of the leaders. Lacazette was our late scorer in an enthralling encounter at Emirates Stadium. We booked our place in the knock out stages of the Europa League with a goalless draw against Sporting, but the evening was marred by a serious injury to Welbeck. It proved to be his last appearance for the club.

Henrikh Mkhitaryan salvaged a late draw at home to Wolves, while Aubameyang was the hero as we got back to winning ways at Bournemouth. We rounded off the month with another victory in Europe. Youngsters Smith Rowe and Joe Willock were both on the scoresheet – the latter for the first time for the senior team.

➚ Arsenal.com Player of the Month
Lucas Torreira

10

DECEMBER

RESULTS

Day	Competition	Opponent	Score
Sun 2	Premier League	**Tottenham Hotspur** (H)	4-2
		Aubameyang 2, Lacazette, Torreira	
Wed 5	Premier League	**Manchester United** (A)	2-2
		Mustafi, Rojo (og)	
Sat 8	Premier League	**Huddersfield Town** (H)	1-0
		Torreira	
Thur 13	Europa League	**Qarabag** (H)	1-0
		Lacazette	
Sun 16	Premier League	**Southampton** (A)	2-3
		Mkhitaryan 2	
Wed 19	Carabao Cup	**Tottenham Hotspur** (H)	0-2
Sat 22	Premier League	**Burnley** (H)	3-1
		Aubameyang 2, Iwobi	
Wed 26	Premier League	**Brighton** (A)	1-1
		Aubameyang	
Sat 29	Premier League	**Liverpool** (A)	1-5
		Maitland-Niles	

We began December with one of our most impressive performances all season – in the north London derby at the Emirates.

Trailing 2-1 at half-time, the Gunners produced an inspirational second-half display to run out 4-2 winners. Torreira sealed the victory with his first goal for the club, celebrating the occasion in jubilant style. The win moved us above our neighbours, into the top four.

Despite twice leading at Old Trafford we were pegged back and had to settle for a draw in the next game against Manchester United three days later, but we ended the week on a high thanks to Torreira's late winner at home to Huddersfield. For all our good form, we had, incredibly, still not led at half-time at all in the Premier League.

The unbeaten run stretched to 22 games in all competitions with a 1-0 win over Qarabag to round off the Europa League group stage and secure top spot. It was the joint-third longest undefeated run in the club's history.

But it all came to an end at St Mary's, where Mkhitaryan's brace wasn't enough to prevent defeat to Southampton.

Elimination in the Carabao Cup followed, before we got back to winning ways with a comfortable defeat of Burnley. The year ended in disappointment though – a single point away to Brighton was followed by a thumping defeat at Anfield, despite Ainsley Maitland-Niles giving us the lead with his first senior goal for the club.

JANUARY

We began 2019 in fifth place, and consolidated our position with a straightforward win over Fulham on New Year's Day.

Attention switched to the FA Cup for a trip to Blackpool and young academy product Willock was the man of the moment – the teenage midfielder scored twice in a 3-0 win at Bloomfield Road. The cup run never really got going though, we fell to Manchester United in the fourth round. Before that we played two London derbies, with contrasting outcomes. A disappointing defeat at West Ham was followed by an excellent 2-0 home win over Chelsea. The only blot on the afternoon was a knee injury picked up by Hector Bellerin that ended his season. Added to the serious injury that Rob Holding suffered the previous month, it meant the defensive options available to Emery were now severely restricted.

Going forward though we continued to look impressive, with both Aubameyang and Lacazette regularly among the goals. Both netted in the win over Cardiff, and the latter claimed the Arsenal.com Player of the Month award for January.

RESULTS

Tue 1	Premier League	**Fulham** (H)	4-1
		Xhaka, Lacazette, Ramsey, Aubameyang	
Sat 5	FA Cup	**Blackpool** (A)	3-0
		Willock 2, Iwobi	
Sat 12	Premier League	**West Ham United** (A)	0-1
Sat 19	Premier League	**Chelsea** (H)	2-0
		Lacazette, Koscielny	
Fri 25	FA Cup	**Manchester United** (H)	1-3
		Aubameyang	
Tue 29	Premier League	**Cardiff City** (H)	2-1
		Aubameyang, Lacazette	

FEBRUARY

Our top-four hopes were dealt a blow with defeat at Manchester City, but we bounced back well to take maximum points in our next three league games in February – Lacazette scored in all three, with Mkhitaryan also impressing. The Europa League campaign resumed with a knock-out tie against BATE Borisov of Belarus. We were hot favourites going into the two-legged affair, having beaten BATE comfortably last season, but we suffered a shock 1-0 reverse in the away leg, putting us under pressure for the Emirates return. It was plain sailing back in London though, from the moment the visitors scored an early own goal. Shkodran Mustafi and Sokratis were also on target to complete the comeback and book our place in the last 16 again.

RESULTS

Sun 3	Premier League	**Manchester City** (A)	**1-3**
		Koscielny	
Sat 9	Premier League	**Huddersfield Town** (A)	**2-1**
		Iwobi, Lacazette	
Thur 14	Europa League	**BATE Borisov** (A)	**0-1**
Thur 21	Europa League	**BATE Borisov** (H)	**3-0**
		Volkov (og), Mustafi, Sokratis	
Sun 24	Premier League	**Southampton** (H)	**2-0**
		Lacazette, Mkhitaryan	
Wed 27	Premier League	**Bournemouth** (H)	**5-1**
		Ozil, Mkhitaryan, Koscielny, Aubameyang, Lacazette	

MARCH

A missed penalty at the end of the north London derby at Wembley Stadium meant we had to settle for a single point, and the resulting draw looked even more costly at the end of the season. Aaron Ramsey had given us a deserved lead in the first half, but Harry Kane struck a controversial penalty to equalise. Bernd Leno had earlier made a tremendous double save to deny Christian Eriksen and then Moussa Sissoko. It looked as though there would be a further twist late on, when Aubameyang won a penalty of his own in the last minute. Our top scorer saw his spot kick saved though, meaning we dropped out of the top four. Worse was to come in France the following week – we lost 3-1 away to Rennes in the first leg of our Europa League tie, having looked comfortable at 1-0 up. Sokratis was sent off late in the first half though, and things began to unravel. We warmed up for the second leg with a memorable Premier League win over Manchester United, and duly pulled off the comeback against Rennes with a 3-0 win at Emirates Stadium. Aubameyang claimed two of the goals, celebrating his second with a Black Panther mask in front of the Clock End.

RESULTS

Sat 2	Premier League	**Tottenham Hotspur** (A) _Ramsey_	1-1
Thur 7	Europa League	**Rennes** (A) _Iwobi_	1-3
Sun 10	Premier League	**Manchester United** (H) _Xhaka, Aubameyang_	2-0
Thur 14	Europa League	**Rennes** (H) _Aubameyang 2, Maitland-Niles_	3-0

15

APRIL

We continued our good run into April, and a 2-0 home win over Newcastle moved us back above Tottenham into third place in the Premier League. But with seven games remaining there were only three points separating the four teams between third and sixth.

Our away form was still a concern though – evidenced by a limp 1-0 defeat at Goodison Park.

There were no such troubles in Europe – Ramsey's last ever Arsenal goal and an own goal from Kalidou Koulibaly ensured an excellent 2-0 home win in the first leg of the quarter-final against a strong Napoli side. Aubameyang's quick-thinking forced a mistake from Watford keeper Ben Foster back in the league, and earned a rare away win, achieved with our only clean sheet on the road in the Premier League all season. We were well placed halfway through the month – both domestically and in Europe, after booking our place in the semi-final with an impressive second leg win in Italy.

But that's when the campaign well and truly hit the skids. A surprise 3-2 reverse to Crystal Palace – our first league defeat at Emirates Stadium since the opening day – was followed by further damaging losses at Wolves and Leicester City. Those three consecutive defeats, and nine goals conceded, saw us crash out of the top four, with just two games left.

RESULTS

Mon 1	Premier League	**Newcastle United** (H)	**2-0**
		Ramsey, Lacazette	
Sun 7	Premier League	**Everton** (A)	**0-1**
Thur 11	Europa League	**Napoli** (H)	**2-0**
		Ramsey, Koulibaly (og)	
Mon 15	Premier League	**Watford** (A)	**1-0**
		Aubameyang	
Thur 18	Europa League	**Napoli** (A)	**1-0**
		Lacazette	
Sun 21	Premier League	**Crystal Palace** (H)	**2-3**
		Ozil, Aubameyang	
Wed 24	Premier League	**Wolves** (A)	**1-3**
		Soktratis	
Sun 28	Premier League	**Leicester City** (A)	**0-3**

↗ **Arsenal.com Player of the Season**

Alexandre Lacazette

MAY

Further dropped points – in a 1-1 draw with Brighton in our final home game of the season meant that our only route to Champions League qualification was now through winning the Europa League. Valencia stood between us and the final, but the deadly striking duo of Lacazette and Aubameyang were far too strong for the Spanish giants. Lacazette – later voted our Player of the Season – scored twice in the first leg win at Emirates Stadium, while his strike partner stole the show in the return in Spain. The Gabon international netted a sensational hat-trick in the intimidating Mestalla on a memorable night, to send us to our first European final for 13 years.

Before that though, there was time for Aubameyang to claim the Premier League Golden Boot award. He scored twice in the final day win at Burnley to take his final tally to 22 in his first full season in English football. Young striker Eddie Nketiah claimed his first Premier

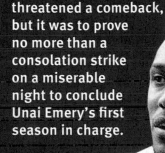

↗ Arsenal.com
Goal of the Season
Pierre-Emerick Aubameyang v
Leicester City (H)

League goal right at the death. And so to Baku, Azerbaijan to take on Chelsea in the Europa League final. The first half was a cagey affair, though we had a couple of good openings. Former Gunners striker Olivier Giroud broke the deadlock early in the second period, and we never recovered. Alex Iwobi's fantastic volley briefly threatened a comeback, but it was to prove no more than a consolation strike on a miserable night to conclude Unai Emery's first season in charge.

RESULTS

Thur 2	Europa League	**Valencia** (H)	3-1
		Lacazette 2, Aubameyang	
Sun 5	Premier League	**Brighton** (H)	1-1
		Aubameyang	
Thur 9	Europa League	**Valencia** (A)	4-2
		Aubameyang 3, Lacazette	
Sun 12	Premier League	**Burnley** (A)	3-1
		Aubameyang 2, Nketiah	
Wed 29	Europa League	**Chelsea** (N)	1-4
		Iwobi	

THE MAN WITH THE GOLDEN BOOT!

Premier League
Golden Boot winner 2018/19
Cadbury

Pierre-Emerick's first full season in English football ended with the striker winning the Golden Boot award for the Premier League's top scorer.

The Gabon international scored 22 goals from 36 appearances during the campaign, to share the award with Liverpool duo Mohamed Salah and Sadio Mane – though our forward played at least 300 fewer minutes than either of those two.

It is the first time we have had the top scorer in the league since 2011/12 when Robin van Persie led the charts, and it's the 12th time overall we have had the top flight's top marksman – no club has won the award more times.

Here are some of the stats around a fantastic season from our formidable front man.

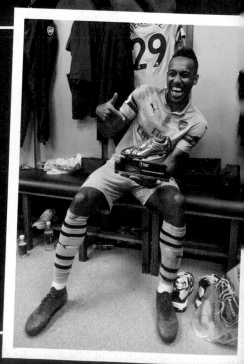

18

When scored

1-15 minutes	5
16-30 minutes	0
31-45 minutes	0
46-60 minutes	6
61-75 minutes	7
76-90 minutes	4

Where scored

Home	13
Away	9

How scored

Right foot	20
Left foot	2

Who scored against

Burnley	4
Fulham	3
Bournemouth	2
Brighton & Hove Albion	2
Cardiff City	2
Crystal Palace	2
Leicester City	2
Tottenham Hotspur	2
Everton	1
Manchester United	1
Watford	1

Auba's goals came once every 124 minutes.

He had 40 shots on target in the Premier League.

He scored 31 goals in all competitions.

As well as 22 goals he added five assists.

His 22 goals included four penalties, and two goals from outside the area.

Five of his goals were set up by Alexandre Lacazette.

ARSENAL'S GOLDEN BOOTS

Player	Season	Goals
Ted Drake	1934/35	42
Ronnie Rooke	1947/48	33
Malcolm Macdonald	1976/77	25
Alan Smith	1988/89	23
Alan Smith	1990/91	22
Ian Wright	1991/92	24
Thierry Henry	2001/02	24
Thierry Henry	2003/04	30
Thierry Henry	2004/05	25
Thierry Henry	2005/06	27
Robin van Persie	2011/12	30
Pierre Emerick-Aubameyang	2018/19	22

MOST GOLDEN BOOTS

ARSENAL	12
EVERTON	12
TOTTENHAM	11
LIVERPOOL	10
SUNDERLAND	8
ASTON VILLA	7
CHELSEA	7
DERBY COUNTY	7
MANCHESTER UNITED	7

OUR TOP SCORERS IN THE PREMIER LEAGUE ERA

1992/93	Ian Wright	15
1993/94	Ian Wright	23
1994/95	Ian Wright	18
1995/96	Ian Wright	15
1996/97	Ian Wright	23
1997/98	Dennis Bergkamp	16
1998/99	Nicolas Anelka	17
1999/00	Thierry Henry	17
2000/01	Thierry Henry	17
2001/02	Thierry Henry	24
2002/03	Thierry Henry	24
2003/04	Thierry Henry	30
2004/05	Thierry Henry	25
2005/06	Thierry Henry	27
2006/07	Robin van Persie	11
2007/08	Emmanuel Adebayor	24
2008/09	Robin van Persie	11
2009/10	Cesc Fabregas	15
2010/11	Robin van Persie	18
2011/12	Robin van Persie	30
2012/13	Theo Walcott	14
2013/14	Olivier Giroud	16
2014/15	Alexis Sanchez	16
2015/16	Olivier Giroud	16
2016/17	Alexis Sanchez	24
2017/18	Alexandre Lacazette	14
2018/19	Pierre-Emerick Aubameyang	22

MEMORY LANE

Our players take a trip back in time, way back to early in their lives, before they signed for the Gunners...

When did you first want to become a footballer?

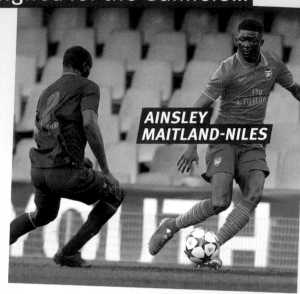

AINSLEY MAITLAND-NILES

Pierre-Emerick Aubameyang
Well I know it was a very long time ago! I was three years old I think, when I first went to the stadium to watch a game. My father was playing for Le Havre, so I went to the stadium to watch him. I enjoyed it a lot. It was from that moment that I knew I wanted to be a football player.

Rob Holding
When I was younger I was just playing football because I liked it, that's why you played. It wasn't until I was about 14 or 15 when it started to be an option after school that I realised I could make a career out of it.

Sokratis
I was very young, I think about nine years old. That's when I started playing for a small kids' team. But I liked football before that. I started playing small-sided games at that age, five-a-side or six-a-side.

Ainsley Maitland-Niles
I'd say it was around the age of four. It was either football or basketball, and I chose football, maybe because my older brother played it.

Granit Xhaka
I was very young. The first time I was on the pitch was when I was four. My Dad wanted to go into the sport, so that's why I started playing football as a hobby.

Mesut Ozil
I was six or seven years old when I wanted to start playing football. I always used to watch the games with my brother. At that time I wasn't thinking about professional football though, I just wanted to play with my friends, my family – for fun. Afterwards I worked hard, trained hard, to become a professional.

Bernd Leno
I joined a club when I was six years old in the small town of Bietigheim-Bissingen, which is where I grew up in the south of Germany, near Stuttgart. I lived there with my brother, mother and father. 50,000 people live there, I still have many friends there and my family still live there, I think after my career I'll come back to that small town again.

MESUT OZIL

VICTORIA
versichert

What is the most memorable game from your youth?

Aubameyang

I remember a lot of games from when I was growing up, but one especially. We were winning 1-0, but I hadn't scored. Then I saw my grandpa was watching the game, and I thought 'Now I have to score'. Then I did – with a bicycle kick! I was really happy. I think I was nine years old at the time.

Ozil

I was always the youngest one in the team, and usually the smallest one. If you saw me you would think I was much younger, but when we played the tournaments, I was so good, and scored a lot of goals, that often the parents of kids on the other teams would say I was older than I said I was! They didn't believe me! But I always loved the tournaments, I was often voted the best player and was the top scorer. When I was about eight I remember playing against Schalke 04, when I

PIERRE-EMERICK AUBAMEYANG

was at the smallest club in Gelsenkirchen. We reached the final of a tournament against them, and nobody had even scored against Schalke, never mind beaten them. We were a really small club, but after two minutes I scored. The whole crowd was stunned. I remember it well, the atmosphere was crazy after that. Nobody had scored against them before, until I did. I honestly don't remember whether we won or lost, but to score against them was a big moment.

Lacazette

I can remember playing in a tournament where my team were losing – I came off the bench and we won 4-1.

Sokratis

We played every week, I can't remember a specific game, but we played every Saturday and I used to really look forward to the matches, after training all week. I really loved it, every game.

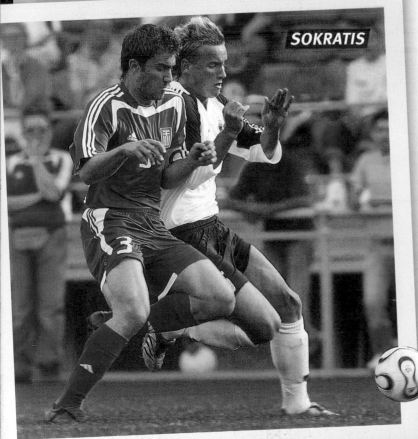

SOKRATIS

Did you ever play any other position when you were younger?

ROB HOLDING

Aubameyang
No, no. I always wanted to score goals, so I was always a striker.

Leno
First I was a midfielder, but when I was seven our goalkeeper didn't come to the tournament one time. The coach asked us all who wanted to be the goalkeeper. I said 'I want to try' and it was very good. Then my parents bought me some gloves and I never wanted to leave the goal!

Holding
Back then I played seven-a-side so we had two at the back – I was a right back and a centre half together. I always remained on that side of the halfway line! I'd say it's quite similar to now in that I'd play it quite simple and I didn't really try to do much. When I was at my local team I'd do everything, but when I went to Bolton there was a structure to it and I had to pass to other people and let them create things and score goals. I was very much at the back and steady. I've made a career out of being steady! I was always a bit taller than my team-mates, but when I got to high school there were some really tall kids and I was just under them. I've always been above average.

Sokratis
I played in midfield, and also up front when I was younger. I was bigger than the rest of the kids my age. I started there, but when I joined the young national team – at under-13 level I think – they changed my position and I started to play as a defender.

Xhaka
I started as a striker. I was really small and enjoyed playing up front.

Guendouzi
I started off as a forward but as time passed I've gradually moved further back into midfield.

Lacazette
I was an attacking midfielder then I became a striker.

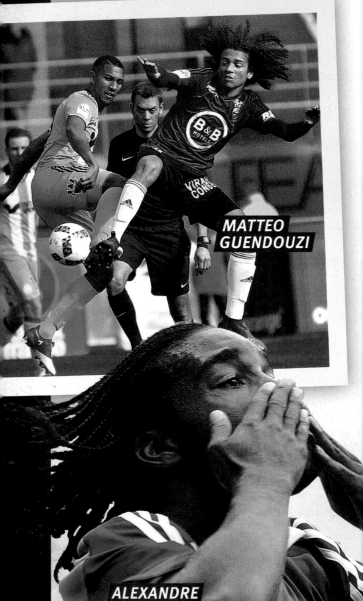

MATTEO GUENDOUZI

ALEXANDRE LACAZETTE

Are there any similarities in your playing style now, to when you started as a youngster?

GRANIT XHAKA

Aubameyang

I was quick! I've always been quick and everybody told me that you're always quick, but when I got a bit older, like 15 or 16, I had some problems with my knees so I wasn't as fast. But then I worked a lot on my speed when I was at AC Milan and then I became quick again.

Holding

Well I always try and just stay relaxed about it. I don't work myself up too much because that's when you make mistakes. I always had this laidback attitude of whatever will happen, will happen and it's how you react to it. You can't control every aspect of the game and you've got to let it happen. I've always had that approach and it will probably stay.

Xhaka

I think I was young mentally before I became a pro. You change a lot and now you're older you can improve every day and every year. I am happy. I'm happy with my career and my life and those are the important things.

was playing in the cage that I could see things that other people couldn't. They were always amazed by it. That has always been there for me, I didn't learn it, I always had it. Thanks to God I have that ability, and it's so important to see things quickly in football because you get no time on the ball. Even 10 years ago you had more time to think, but now the game is even faster, and you have to make quick decisions and have that instinct.

Guendouzi

As a young kid I scored a lot more goals since I used to play as a forward. Of course, I score far fewer these days.

Ozil

Well what is the same is my instincts. I don't know if you would call it my vision or what, but I always had that. People used to say when I

BERND LENO

Lacazette

I've developed in my way of thinking. I think more about teamwork now, how I can help the team. I take my role as 'the first defender' more seriously. But I think I've developed in every attribute.

23

INSTA HEROES

Let's take a look at what our players have been getting up to on Instagram lately...

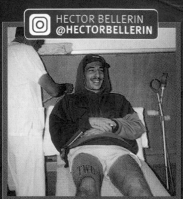

HECTOR BELLERIN
@HECTORBELLERIN

February 20, 2019
So far so good. It's starting to look like a knee again 😐

AINSLEY MAITLAND-NILES
@AINS_MN

December 22, 2018
3 points ... early Christmas present ⚫⚪

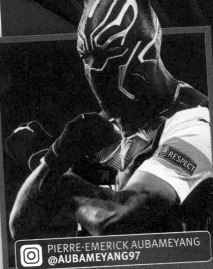

PIERRE-EMERICK AUBAMEYANG
@AUBAMEYANG97

March 14, 2019
❌ **Panther** ❌

ROB HOLDING
@RHOLDING95

March 26, 2019
Rehab in Dubai ain't too shabby 👊

SHKODRAN MUSTAFI
@SHKODRANMUSTAFI

March 15, 2019
⬅️➡️⬆️ **TEAMSPIRIT** 🔥 **#sm20**
#alwaysbelieve
📷 **by @stuart_photoafc** 👏

EDDIE NKETIAH
@EDDIENKETIAH

March 23, 2019
Enjoy every goal like it's my first! #Golazo 😂😂😂

24

SEND KOLASINAC
@SEADK6

January 6, 2019
🚀👊 #SeoKol

BERND LENO
@BERNDLENO1

June 15, 2019
Road trip through 🇺🇸

ALEXANDRE LACAZETTE
@LACAZETTEALEX

May 21, 2019
⭐ LEGEND ✨

MESUT OZIL
@M10_OFFICIAL

June 7, 2019
Mrs. & Mr. Özil
👰🖤🤵

GRANIT XHAKA
@GRANITXHAKA

March 21, 2019
This kid is always smiling and when he smiles, you have to smile as well 😊 @julian_prinz_2010 #WorldDownSyndromeDay

LUCAS TORREIRA
@LTORREIRA34

May 31, 2019
Surely in my life I will fall a lot of times, but I have clear in my mind one thing. I'm going to continue fighting and trying to achieve my dreams. Proud of this team. Thanks to the fans for their love during the whole season. We will come back stronger than ever. Come On Gunners 🖤

MATTEO GUENDOUZI
@MATTEOGUENDOUZI

May 9, 2019
Let's go to the FINAL 🔥🔥🔥
Amazing performance Guys 💪⚫⚪
#COYG @europaleague @arsenal

SOKRATIS PAPASTATHOPOULOS
@SOKRATISPAPA.OFFICIAL

December 2, 2018

BEHIND THE SCENES
AT THE ARSENAL TRAINING CENTRE

The Arsenal Training Centre is the day-to-day headquarters of the club. While matchday is all about Emirates Stadium, the rest of the week it's our training centre in Hertfordshire that's the hub of the action. The players train here of course, but also wind down, relax, rehabilitate, dine together, analyse performances and lots more besides. And it's not just the first-team, the site is also home to the full-time youth team players, as well as the title-winning women's team.

The facilities manager is Sean O'Connor, so we asked him to show us round the impressive site.

FIRST-TEAM DRESSING ROOM

"This is the players' sanctuary, the place where they relax, socialise, can be together without any outside distractions. The room is designed so that you have eye contact with team-mates at all times.

"We want to make it as comfortable as possible for the players, and that is reflected in the colour scheme and the lighting for example. We want the players to be at ease and relaxed, because that's what the training ground is all about. It's about preparation and recovery, so the state of mind is about being relaxed. Then when you get to Emirates Stadium you see more dominant red colours and that's about getting people ready for the contest.

"Every player in the first-team squad has his own locker in the changing room, and they sit in squad number order. Only one player in 20 years ever changed position - that was Robert Pires who wanted to be next to Thierry Henry.

"It's important that the changing room helps to create a team spirit and camaraderie and that's what everything is geared towards. No matter how many decades you go back, the environment of the dressing room is what helps create winning teams".

PITCHES

"There are 11 pitches on site, with seven of them made to exactly the same spec as the Emirates Stadium playing surface. The pitches are looked after by head groundsman Steve Braddock and his team of 18, and they are all completely renovated every season.

"There are three pitches for each age group, and the 10th pitch is our dedicated match pitch, with sponsorship boards, etc. which you may have seen if you have watched youth games on Arsenal Player.

"This is the George Armstrong memorial pitch, where the under-18s play home games on Saturdays.

"The 11th pitch is a rougher area that can be used to replicate specific conditions.

"As well as the regular training sessions, the fitness coaches will use outdoor areas, and there are two dedicated goalkeeping coaching areas too. They have a slightly different pitch construction, they are a bit springier to help with the guys diving around".

INDOOR SPORTS HALL

"Our indoor 3G field turf pitch, measures 60 by 50 metres in size. This is used sometimes when the weather is particularly bad, but not very often. Media work is sometimes carried out here as well, so you might see it on our YouTube channel".

BOOTROOM

"This is where the players' tools of their trade are housed. After getting changed, the players go to the disrobing room where kitmen, Paul Akers and Will Jones, will be waiting for them because they may want a choice of boots for that day's training. The players' boots are all kept here, including match boots - the players don't take them home with them.

"At the end of the training session before each matchday, the players will select their boots for the game. For home matchdays they know what the Emirates pitch is like, and they will tend to take two pairs each: one pair of moulds, one pair of studs. For away games they might take as many as three or four pairs each, then see what conditions are like when they arrive.

"So that means there are hundreds of boots kept in our boot room. The players each have an average of six pairs of boots at any one

time, and when you consider there are about 30 players in the first-team squad, that's a lot of boots.

"Players tend to change their boots more often now than in the past. Someone like Dennis Bergkamp, for example, used to wear the same pair of boots all season. The days of the kitmen taking boots to the cobblers on Highbury Hill are well gone! The individual boot sponsors can also have a say in when players should change boots.

"The boot room is traditionally a focal point, an informal meeting place, for players and staff alike. That has never changed. Kitmen, whether they have been in the job for one year or 50 years, always have a great sense of comradery. Wherever you go in football, the friendliness of kitmen is always apparent".

POOL AREA

"Used mainly for rehab purposes, the pool has a movable floor so the physios and fitness staff can select the depth they require.

"We have an indoor shoe policy here, which means everyone changes their footwear when they come into the building. The players change theirs just inside the reception area, before heading through to the changing room.

"The pool is just the other side of the changing room, and other facilities on that side of the building include massage rooms, Jacuzzi, ice bath and steam room".

GYM

"This is a relatively new addition to the training ground, and is the result of years of research. It really is state of the art, with all of the latest equipment available. It's paperless as well, all data is captured digitally on tablets".

MEDICAL BUILDING

"We added the medical building to the site in October 2011.

"The idea behind the facility is that it's much more effective to work with players on an individual basis, and it allowed the medical staff to take this work away from the shared gym in the main building.

"It's completely bespoke, there are two rubber surfaces, one for a running track, to create different balance environments.

"The equipment is also very specialist, such as AlterG anti-gravity treadmills. As it's separated from the main building, it also helps create a desire for the player to recover quickly and join the rest of the group in the main gym. So we find it helps to mentally stimulate players as well.

"The medical building is used every single day, by all members of the first-team squad, the women's team and also youth players with long-term injuries. It's a seven-day-a-week building, not just for injured players, but also those who want to tailor their warm-ups and routines".

DECOR/INTERIOR

"Over the past few months we have made a conscious effort to update and improve the decor and branding around the whole facility, with a mixture of inspirational and motivating messages and imagery".

BRIEFING ROOM

"This is where team meetings take place. A nice touch here is the list of every single player to have represented the first-team – more than 125 years of Arsenal history. At the start of this season that list had 864 names on it".

EPPC OFFICES

"The Elite Players' Performance building hosts the gym, but also plenty of offices, and a boardroom where our young players sign their first pro contracts. The staff based here include our scouts and analysts".

SLEEP ROOM

"This is used usually if the team arrive back into the country late after an away game - usually in Europe - and staff or players want to sleep before driving home. The sleep room has 11 beds".

WOMEN'S HUB

"The WSL champions are based downstairs in the media building but that's mainly where their admin hub is - they actually use most of the facilities of the training ground.

"They train five days a week and have access to all of the facilities, as well as their own changing room and office areas".

RESTAURANT

"The players' restaurant and kitchens are situated upstairs, above the main entrance foyer, and overlook the pitches, with large windows which run the entire length of the room. We have long tables for the players to dine at, and the kitchen staff will often serve as many as 300 covers each day, as it's used by all the playing staff, from full-time academy players upwards.

"The youth players sit at one end of the room, the first-team players at the other. Though there are no physical barriers in place, the ethos at the club is that the young players can see a path up to the first-team area.

"We serve lunch between 12pm and 2.30pm and mobile phones are banned between these times.

"Christian Sandhagen is the team chef, and he is joined by two more chefs and five kitchen staff".

MEDIA BUILDING

"Unai Emery gives a press conference here before every game, so often twice a week during the season.

"The media room has a retractable door so we can accommodate at least 100 people. In addition we have seven individual interview rooms for one-to-one filmed interviews. The outside broadcast trucks are situated in the car park to the front, so television companies can broadcast live from here.

"This building also contains several offices and a restaurant that's used by staff and the women's team".

CLASSROOMS

"There are two bespoke classrooms on site, for the education of the academy players. They have school sessions three times a week".

LAUNDRY

"All of our laundry is done here on site, and as you can imagine, there's a huge lot to get turned round every day - approximately 300 kits on a busy day".

SPOT THE DIFFERENCE

See if you can spot the 10 differences between these two pictures

Answers on page 61

GAPS IN YOUR KNOWLEDGE?

Here are some of our most memorable games from last season, but are there any gaps in your knowledge?

Q	Date	Opposition	Venue	Competition	Score	First Arsenal scorer
1	7/10/2018	Fulham	Craven Cottage	Premier League	?	Lacazette
2	22/10/2018	Leicester City	?	Premier League	3-1	Ozil
3	2/12/2018	Tottenham	Emirates Stadium	Premier League	4-2	?
4	5/1/2019	Blackpool	Bloomfield Road	?	3-0	Willock
5	19/1/2019	Chelsea	Emirates Stadium	Premier League	2-0	?
6	27/2/2019	?	Emirates Stadium	Premier League	5-1	Ozil
7	10/3/2019	Manchester United	Emirates Stadium	?	2-0	Xhaka
8	14/3/2019	Rennes	Emirates Stadium	Europa League	?	Aubameyang
9	18/4/2019	Napoli	?	Europa League	1-0	Lacazette
10	9/5/2019	?	Mestalla Stadium	Europa League	4-2	Aubameyang

Answers on page 61

31

KITTED OUT

Adidas are back as our kit manufacturers, and have produced three amazing kits for season 2019/20. But how would the kit look if YOU could design it? Try it out here, using Gunnersaurus as your model!

= ADI-FACTS! =

• Adidas made our kit previously between 1986 and 1994.

• We won six trophies in that time, including two league titles.

• George Graham was our manager back then.

• Alan Smith won the Golden Boot twice in that time, and Ian Wright once.

WHO SCORED MORE?

Out of the following pairs of players, who scored more often for the Gunners?

1

Marc Overmars or
Nicklas Bendtner?

2

Andrey Arshavin
Samir Nasri?

3

Alexis Sanchez or
Robert Pires?

4

Robin van Persie
Dennis Bergkamp?

5

Cesc Fabregas or
Aaron Ramsey?

6

Patrick Vieira
Santi Cazorla?

7

Ray Parlour or
Tomas Rosicky?

8

Lukas Podolski
Eduardo?

9

Paul Merson or
Olivier Giroud?

10

Gilberto
Abou Diaby?

Answers on page 61

CHAMPIONS!

Arsenal Women were the toast of English football last season, winning the FA Women's Super League title for the first time since 2012, finishing seven points ahead of Manchester City after an unforgettable campaign. There were stellar performances across the squad, but star striker Vivianne Miedema took most of the headlines, winning the Golden Boot award with 22 goals from her 20 WSL appearances. The Netherlands international scored three hat-tricks during the campaign, and also added 10 assists. She scored 31 goals in all competitions, with Danielle van de Donk, Kim Little and Katie McCabe also reaching double figures for Joe Montemurro's free-flowing side.

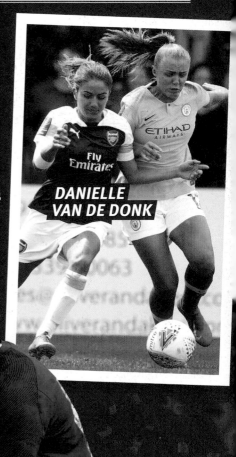

DANIELLE VAN DE DONK

and new signing Jill Roord helped the Dutch to the final, where they lost 2-0 to USA.

Goalkeeper Pauline Peyraud-Magnin played for host nation France, while Leah Williamson and Beth Mead were in Phil Neville's England side that reached the semi-final. Little, Lisa Evans and Jennifer Beattie featured for Scotland, while Leonie Maier played for Germany.

This was our 15th league title overall, extending our record as the most successful women's team in English football. Since foundation in 1987 Arsenal Women FC have now won 44 major honours, and this season will have another crack at the Women's Champions League, which we lifted in 2007.

In the summer, 10 of our championship-winning side starred at the World Cup in France – with three reaching the final with the Netherlands. Miedema, Van de Donk

JILL ROORD

BETH MEAD

FINAL 2019 FAWSL TABLE

Team	P	W	D	L	F	A	GD	Pts
1. Arsenal	20	18	0	2	70	13	57	54
2. Manchester City	20	14	5	1	53	17	36	47
3. Chelsea	20	12	6	2	46	14	32	42
4. Birmingham City	20	13	1	6	29	17	12	40
5. Reading	20	8	3	9	33	30	3	27
6. Bristol City	20	7	4	9	17	34	-17	25
7. West Ham United	20	7	2	11	25	37	-12	23
8. Liverpool	20	7	1	12	21	38	-17	22
9. Brighton & Hove Albion	20	4	4	12	16	38	-22	16
10. Everton	20	3	3	14	15	38	-23	12
11. Yeovil Town	20	2	1	17	11	60	-49	-3

JOE MONTEMURRO ON WINNING THE LEAGUE

"It means a lot because we've had an interesting year. They've come together as a group and there's been a lot of adversity with regards to the injuries and so on. As a group, the love and the respect they have for each other really culminates in what we've achieved.

"I've got a bit of an emotional twinge. To coach an Arsenal team to a championship as an Arsenal fan is mind-boggling. It's something I'd never have thought about growing up and becoming a coach. I'm very proud and very honoured to be here as an Arsenal coach."

PLAYER PROFILES

1
GK

BERND LENO

26
GK

EMILIANO MARTINEZ

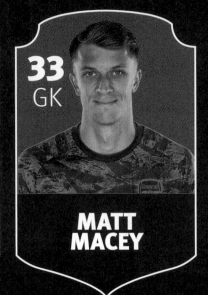

33
GK

MATT MACEY

German stopper Bernd enjoyed a hugely impressive debut season with the Gunners, pulling off a string of fantastic saves after working his way into the team in late September. Having joined from Bundesliga side Bayer Leverkusen, the Germany international soon began to show his worth, looking confident with the ball at his feet as well as demonstrating excellent reactions, most notably when he made an incredible double save in the north London derby at Wembley. He won the Under-17 Euros in 2009 before lifting the 2017 Confederations Cup with the senior national team.

Born: Bietigheim-Bissingen, Germany, Mar 4, 1992
Joined Arsenal: from Bayer Leverkusen on June 19, 2018
Previous clubs: Stuttgart, Bayer Leverkusen
Arsenal debut: v Vorskla Poltava (h), Europa League, Sept 20, 2018

Agile keeper Emi impressed while on loan at Reading in the Championship last season, finishing fourth in their Player of the Season poll, despite only joining for the second half of the campaign. He played just once for the Gunners in 2018/19, keeping a clean sheet in the Europa League group stage win at home to Qarabag. Full name Damian Emiliano Martinez, the Argentina youth international is now in his eighth season with the Gunners, though has spent large periods away on loan. He has an enviable clean sheet ratio of one in every two appearances.

Born: Buenos Aires, Argentina, Sept 2, 1992
Joined Arsenal: from Independiente on Aug 1, 2010
Previous clubs: Independiente, Oxford Utd (loan), Sheff Wed (loan), Rotherham Utd (loan), Wolves (loan), Reading (loan)
Arsenal debut: v Coventry City (h), League Cup, Sept 26, 2012

Promoted to the first-team squad last summer, giant keeper Matt spent last season on loan at Plymouth Argyle in League One. He made more than 30 appearances, gaining valuable experience after previous loan spells at Accrington Stanley in 2015 and Luton Town in 2017. Having joined from Bristol Rovers as a teenager in 2013, the goalie made his first-team debut during the 2017/18 season – in a 2-1 Carabao Cup win over Norwich at Emirates Stadium. The following month he kept a clean sheet in a Europa League win over Red Star. At 6ft 7in, Matt is the tallest player ever to represent the first team.

Born: Bath, Sept 9, 1994
Joined Arsenal: from Bristol Rovers on Oct 25, 2013
Previous clubs: Bristol Rovers, Accrington Stanley (loan), Luton Town (loan), Plymouth Argyle (loan)
Arsenal debut: v Norwich City (a), League Cup, Oct 24, 2017

PLAYER PROFILES

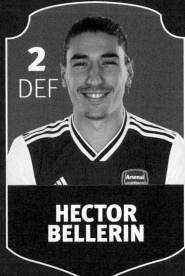

2
DEF

HECTOR BELLERIN

5
DEF

SOKRATIS PAPASTATHOPOULOS

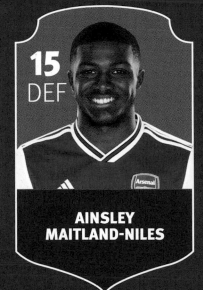

15
DEF

AINSLEY MAITLAND-NILES

One of the fastest players in the entire Premier League, right back Hector missed the second half of last season with a cruciate ligament injury sustained against Chelsea in January 2019. He made his Gunners debut while still a teenager, and has been a regular in the side for the past five years, having joined our academy from home-town club Barcelona aged just 16. Also comfortable at wing back, Hector is excellent going forward, and has more than 20 assists to his name so far. A full international since making his debut in 2016, he was part of Spain's squad at that year's European Championships.

Born: Barcelona, Spain, Mar 19, 1995
Joined Arsenal: as a scholar in summer 2011
Previous club: Watford (loan)
Arsenal debut: v West Brom (a), League Cup, Sept 25, 2013

Imposing and uncompromising central defender Sokratis settled straight into the team during his debut season in London. The Greece international made 40 appearances in all competitions, scoring three times. But it was his defensive work that caught the attention, immediately getting up to speed with the demands of English football to become a crucial part of the Gunners backline. A German Cup winner with previous club Borussia Dortmund in 2017, he had earlier won the Serie A title in Italy with AC Milan. Known simply as Papa around the squad, he was Greek Young Player of the Year in 2007/08.

Born: Kalamata, Greece, June 9, 1988
Joined Arsenal: from Borussia Dortmund on July 2, 2018
Previous clubs: AEK Athens, Niki Volos (loan), Genoa, AC Milan, Werder Bremen, Borussia Dortmund
Arsenal debut: v Manchester City (h), League, Aug 12, 2018

A product of the Arsenal Academy, Ainsley enjoyed a sustained run in the first-team last season, racking up 30 appearances in all, mainly at right wing back. Pacey, determined and with superb powers of recovery, the England youth international scored his first senior goals for the club last season. Also able to play in midfield, the youngster's versatility is a huge benefit to Unai Emery. An Arsenal player from the age of six, he went on loan to Ipswich in the Championship in 2015/16, and was part of the victorious England squad at the 2017 FIFA Under-20 World Cup.

Born: Goodmayes, Aug 29, 1997
Joined Arsenal: as a scholar in summer 2013
Previous club: Ipswich Town (loan)
Arsenal debut: v Galatasaray (a), Champions League, Dec 9, 2014

PLAYER PROFILES

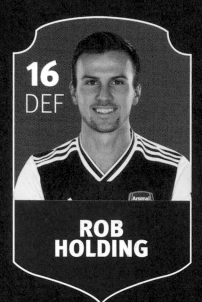

16 DEF

ROB HOLDING

31 DEF

SEAD KOLASINAC

20 DEF

SHKODRAN MUSTAFI

A cruciate ligament injury brought an early end to Rob's season in December 2018, having started the campaign well under Unai Emery. A tough and composed central defender, he has gone from strength to strength since joining from Bolton Wanderers aged just 20. He was named Player of the Season at his previous club in 2015/16, then progressed to the England Under-21 set up, winning the 2016 Toulon Tournament with the Three Lions. Now in his fourth season at the club, he played a big role in winning the 2017 FA Cup final against Chelsea.

Born: Tameside, Sept 20, 1995
Joined Arsenal: from Bolton Wanderers on July 22, 2016
Previous clubs: Bolton Wanderers, Bury (loan)
Arsenal debut: v Liverpool (h), League, Aug 14, 2016

The Bosnia international left back was one of our most creative players last season, contributing seven assists in all competitions and creating 31 goalscoring chances in the Premier League alone. Always looking to dart into opposition territory – whether playing at full back or wing back – the burly defender is now in his third season with the Gunners. He was named in the Bundesliga 2016/17 Team of the Season before joining from FC Schalke, and scored on his Arsenal debut. Although born in Germany, he starred for Bosnia and Herzegovina at the 2014 World Cup.

Born: Karlsruhe, Germany, June 20, 1993
Joined Arsenal: from FC Schalke 04 on June 6, 2017
Previous club: FC Schalke 04
Arsenal debut: v Chelsea (n), Community Shield, Aug 8, 2017

Experienced defender Shkodran passed the 100-appearance mark last season, and has been a regular at the heart of the backline since joining from Valencia at the start of 2016/17 – indeed he was unbeaten in each of his first 22 games for the club. Strong in the tackle and powerful in the air, the centre half made more clearances in the Premier League (161) than any other Arsenal player last season. A member of Germany's 2014 World Cup winning squad, he also won the 2017 Confederations Cup and starred at Euro 2016.

Born: Bad Hersfeld, Germany, Apr 17, 1992
Joined Arsenal: from Valencia on Aug 29, 2016
Previous clubs: Everton, Sampdoria, Valencia
Arsenal debut: v Southampton (h), League, Sept 10, 2016

PLAYER PROFILES

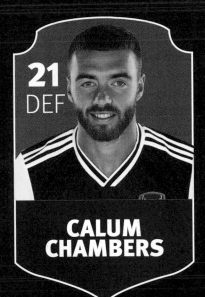

21
DEF

CALUM CHAMBERS

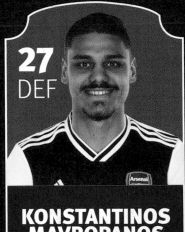

27
DEF

KONSTANTINOS MAVROPANOS

32
MID

EMILE SMITH ROWE

Calum spent the whole of last season on loan to Fulham, and was named their Player of the Season after impressing mainly in a defensive midfield role for the London side. It was his second successful loan spell, having spent 2016/17 at Middlesbrough. He signed a new contract with the Gunners prior to the 2018/19 season, as he approached his 100th Arsenal appearance since joining from Southampton at the age of 19 in 2014. He has played in defence for most of his Gunners career to date, either in the centre or at right back. A full England international, he lifted silverware with England Under-21s in the 2016 Toulon Tournament.

Born: Petersfield, Jan 20, 1995
Joined Arsenal: from Southampton on July 28, 2014
Previous clubs: Southampton, Middlesbrough (loan), Fulham (loan)
Arsenal debut: v Man City (n), Community Shield, Aug 10, 2014

The young Greek defender had his first full season at the club disrupted by injury, but he continued his development with four more first-team outings. A hugely promising central defender, Dinos – as he is known around the club – joined from the Greek league in the 2018 January transfer window, and made his debut at Old Trafford later that season. The 6ft 4in dynamic defender represents his country at under-21 level, and will hope to follow compatriot Sokratis to full international honours as soon as possible.

Born: Athens, Greece, Dec 11, 1997
Joined Arsenal: from PAS Giannina on Jan 4, 2018
Previous club: PAS Giannina
Arsenal debut: v Man United (a), League, Apr 29, 2018

Naturally-gifted attacking midfielder Emile made his breakthrough to the first team last season, before heading to Germany to spend the second half of the campaign at top-flight side RB Leipzig. Another product of the Arsenal academy, the highly-rated youngster is both a creator and scorer of goals, netting three from just six appearances for Unai Emery's side in 2018/19. Skilful on the ball, and a composed finisher, Emile is a player in the modern-style, who is also dangerous from set pieces. An England youth international from under-16 level upwards, he won the Under-17 World Cup with the Three Lions in 2017.

Born: Croydon, July 28, 2000
Joined Arsenal: as a scholar in summer 2016
Previous club: RB Leipzig (loan)
Arsenal debut: v Vorskla Poltava (h), Europa League, Sept 20, 2018

PLAYER PROFILES

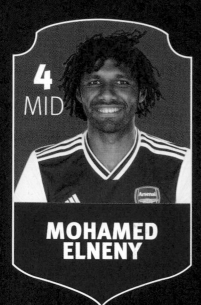

4
MID

MOHAMED ELNENY

7
MID

HENRIKH MKHITARYAN

10
MID

MESUT OZIL

A hard-working yet graceful central midfielder, Mohamed was used sparingly during Unai Emery's first season in charge, but is a dependable presence in the middle of the pitch whenever called upon. His first Gunners goal was a tremendous strike, away to Barcelona, in the 2015/16 Champions League. A mainstay of the Egypt national team, he was a runner-up in the 2017 Africa Cup of Nations, and also played at the 2012 Olympics and 2018 World Cup. He won the league title four years in a row at previous club Basel, where he played alongside close friend Mo Salah. Mohamed will spend this season on loan at Besiktas in Turkey.

Born: El-Mahalla El-Kubra, Egypt, July 11, 1992
Joined Arsenal: from Basel on Jan 14, 2016
Previous clubs: El Mokawloon, Basel
Arsenal debut: v Burnley (h), FA Cup, Jan 30, 2016

The first Armenian to represent Arsenal, attacking midfielder Henrikh scored six times and added seven assists in his first full season at the club last term. Having joined from Manchester United in January 2018, the experienced schemer claimed a hat-trick of assists on his home debut. He continues to link up well with Pierre-Emerick Aubameyang, with whom he had a productive partnership at former club Borussia Dortmund. Named Armenian Footballer of the Year eight times, he is equally at home operating in the number 10 role, or as a wide forward. Henrikh is spending the season on loan at Italian club, Roma.

Born: Yerevan, Armenia, Jan 21, 1989
Joined Arsenal: from Man United on Jan 22, 2018
Previous clubs: Pyunik, Metalurh Donetsk, Shakhtar Donetsk, Borussia Dortmund, Man United
Arsenal debut: v Swansea City (a), League, Jan 30, 2018

Regarded as one of the most creative players in world football, Mesut helped Arsenal return to trophy-winning ways after his record-breaking signing from Real Madrid in 2013. The Gunners won silverware in three of his first four seasons in London, and the playmaker impressed with a string of match-winning performances. In March 2018 he set a new Premier League record for reaching 50 assists faster than any other player in the competition's history. He created more goalscoring chances (45) than any other Arsenal player in the Premier League last term, and scored five goals, from just 20 starts. A World Cup winner with Germany in 2014, he has since retired from international football.

Born: Gelsenkirchen, Germany, Oct 15, 1988
Joined Arsenal: from Real Madrid on Sept 2, 2013
Previous clubs: Schalke, Werder Bremen, Real Madrid
Arsenal debut: v Sunderland (a), League, Sept 14, 2013

PLAYER PROFILES

11
MID

LUCAS TORREIRA

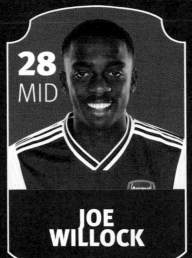

28
MID

JOE WILLOCK

29
MID

MATTEO GUENDOUZI

Tough-tackling Lucas enjoyed a fantastic debut season in London, quickly becoming a fans' favourite with his all-action style. The Uruguay international made 50 appearances in all competitions, scoring a memorable goal in the 4-2 home north London derby victory in December. Voted Arsenal Player of the Month in November, the tenacious central midfielder had spent his whole professional career in Italy's Serie A before joining the Gunners after impressing at the 2018 World Cup. Although only 5ft 6in, Lucas possesses all the required qualities to thrive in the midfield engine room in the Premier League, combining tireless energy with creativity to contribute five assists last term.

Born: Fray Bentos, Uruguay, Feb 11, 1996
Joined Arsenal: from Sampdoria on July 10, 2018
Previous clubs: Pescara, Sampdoria
Arsenal debut: v Manchester City (h), League, August 12, 2018

A box-to-box midfielder with an eye for a goal, Joe scored his first senior goals last season, scoring three times from just six appearances, and continuing his impressive development. Having been part of the Arsenal setup from the age of just four, when he came along to train with older brother Chris, Joe has steadily improved year on year. Formerly a winger or number 10, he now uses his strength and determination to good effect in the centre of the pitch, and the England youth international showed his prowess in front of goal with a brace against Blackpool in the FA Cup third round last term.

Born: London, Aug 20, 1999
Joined Arsenal: as a scholar in summer 2015
Arsenal debut: v Doncaster Rovers (h), League Cup, Sept 20, 2017

Central midfielder Matteo burst onto the scene last season, becoming an important part of Unai Emery's setup while still a teenager. Arriving as a virtual unknown from Lorient in France, he was drafted straight into the team for the opening game of the season, and was a regular from then on. An excellent passer who also enjoys carrying the ball forward, he scored his first Gunners goal in the 3-0 win away to Qarabag in the Europa League. A France youth international, he represented his country at the 2019 European Under-21 Championships.

Born: Poissy, France, Apr 14, 1999
Joined Arsenal: from Lorient on July 11, 2018
Previous clubs: Lorient B, Lorient
Arsenal debut: v Manchester City (h), League, Aug 12, 2018

PLAYER PROFILES

34
MID

GRANIT XHAKA

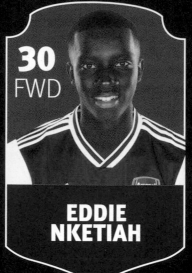

30
FWD

EDDIE NKETIAH

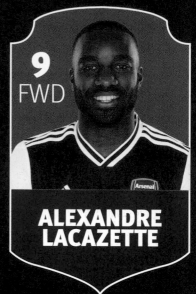

9
FWD

ALEXANDRE LACAZETTE

A natural leader in the heart of the Gunners midfield, Granit has an excellent passing range and a fearsome long-range shot with his powerful left foot. Something of a set-piece specialist, he twice scored direct free-kicks last season, and also contributed five assists. A tireless, hard-working midfielder, he covered more ground than any other Arsenal player in the Premier League last season (322km). A longstanding Switzerland international, he captained his country at the 2019 UEFA Nations League, and scored in the 2018 World Cup. Granit twice won the league title with hometown club Basel.

Born: Basel, Switzerland, Sept 27, 1992
Joined Arsenal: from Borussia Monchengladbach on May 25, 2016
Previous clubs: Basel, Borussia Monchengladbach
Arsenal debut: v Liverpool (h), League, Aug 14, 2016

Another product of our youth system, prolific forward Eddie burst onto the scene in 2017/18 with two late goals to knock Norwich City out of the Carabao Cup at Emirates Stadium. He continued his development last season, and signed off 2018/19 with his first ever Premier League goal, in the final day win at Burnley. A natural finisher, he scored 70 goals at youth level during his first four seasons, and has also netted more than 20 goals for England at under-18 to under-21 levels. He was the top scorer for Arsenal Under-23s last season, and was rewarded by being promoted to the first-team dressing room before the current campaign.

Eddie is spending the season on loan to Leeds United in the Championship.

Born: London, May 30, 1999
Joined Arsenal: as a scholar in summer 2015
Arsenal debut: v BATE Borisov (a), Europa League, Sept 28, 2017

Voted Arsenal Player of the Season for 2018/19, the prolific frontman netted 19 goals in all competitions, forming a deadly partnership up front with close friend Pierre-Emerick Aubameyang. The France international forward led the way in terms of Premier League assists (eight), demonstrating there is much more to the striker's game than goals. Previously with Lyon, he scored exactly 100 league goals for his hometown club, before a then record-breaking transfer to the Gunners in 2017. He scored just 94 seconds into his Premier League debut, against Leicester City at Emirates Stadium.

Born: Lyon, France, May 28, 1991
Joined Arsenal: from Lyon on July 5, 2017
Previous club: Lyon
Arsenal debut: v Chelsea (n), Community Shield, Aug 6, 2017

PLAYER PROFILES

14 FWD

PIERRE-EMERICK AUBAMEYANG

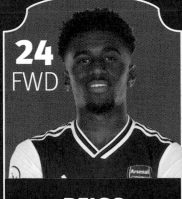

24 FWD

REISS NELSON

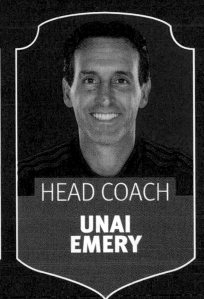

HEAD COACH

UNAI EMERY

With 22 Premier League goals, 'Auba' as he is known around the club, won the Golden Boot award for 2018/19. He took his tally to 31 in all competitions, including a memorable hat-trick in the Europa League semi-final at Valencia. He became our record signing when joining from Borussia Dortmund in early 2018, having scored 141 goals for the German side. A pacey, exhilarating striker, he recorded the top speed of any Arsenal player in the Premier League last season (34.75 km/h), and scored 27 goals with his trusty right foot. A long-standing Gabon international, he was named African Player of the Year in 2015.

Born: Laval, France, June 18, 1989
Joined Arsenal: from Borussia Dortmund on Jan 31, 2018
Previous clubs: AC Milan, Dijon (loan), Lille (loan), Monaco (loan), Saint-Etienne, Borussia Dortmund
Arsenal debut: v Everton (h), League, Feb 3, 2018

Exciting winger Reiss impressed while on loan at Hoffenheim in Germany's Bundesliga last term, breaking their club record for the youngest player to reach seven goals. Able to play on either flank, or behind the striker, the youngster – who has been at Arsenal since the age of 16 – usually operates on the right wing. Fleet-footed and direct, Reiss made his first-team debut when just 17, and is a regular for England's youth teams. He was named in the 2016 European U17 Championships Team of the Tournament, and scored for England at the European U21 Championships in June 2019.

Born: London, Dec 10, 1999
Joined Arsenal: as a scholar in summer 2016
Previous club: Hoffenheim (loan)
Arsenal debut: v Chelsea (n), Community Shield, Aug 6, 2017

Now in his second season at the club, Unai guided Arsenal to our first European final for 13 years in his debut campaign in London. Having lost his first two games in charge after joining from Paris Saint-Germain, he then oversaw a 22-game unbeaten run in all competitions, as he quickly got to grips with English football. He won seven trophies in just two years as boss of Paris SG, having won three successive Europa League trophies while in charge of Sevilla. Unai made his name in the lower leagues in his native Spain, having success at Lorca Deportivo and Almeria before taking over at Valencia, whom he too to three successive top three finishes in La Liga. He was a midfielder in his playing days, until injury forced his retirement in 2004.

Born: Hondarribia, Spain, November 3, 1971
Joined Arsenal: May 23, 2018
Clubs as a player: Real Sociedad B, Real Sociedad, Toledo, Racing Ferrol, Leganes, Lorca Deportivo

NEW PLAYERS

It was a busy pre-season for the club in the transfer market, with new director of football Edu overseeing a number of deals. Here's the lowdown on our six summer signings...

Dani Ceballos
Midfielder

Squad number: 8
Born: Utrera, Spain, August 7, 1996
Joined Arsenal (on loan): from Real Madrid on July 25, 2019

Exciting Spain international midfielder Dani is on loan for the season from Real Madrid. Named player of the tournament at the 2017 European Under-21 Championship, he is graceful, quick, and an excellent dribbler who likes to operate just behind the main forwards, and create chances from midfield. He had spent two years at Real Madrid, having previously starred for Real Betis, and made 23 La Liga appearances for the Madrid side last season, scoring three goals from central midfield. His list of honours is already impressive, winning the European Under-19 and Under-21 Championships with Spain, as well as the Champions League (2017/18), UEFA Super Cup (2017) and FIFA Club World Cup (2017 and 2019) with Real Madrid. Has been a senior Spain international since September 2018.

David Luiz
Defender

Squad number: 23
Born: Diadema, Brazil, April 22, 1987
Joined Arsenal: from Chelsea on
August 8, 2019

Experienced central defender David joined us just before the transfer deadline in August, making the switch from London rivals Chelsea. The Brazil international had spent seven seasons with the Blues over two spells, winning the Champions League (2011/12), Premier League (2016/17), two FA Cups (2011/12, 2017/18) and two Europa Leagues (2012/13, 2018/19). Previously in his illustrious career he was a league title winner at Benfica in Portugal, and twice with Paris Saint-Germain, where he worked under Unai Emery. A flamboyant defender with an excellent eye for a pass and able to build the play from the back, David has also won honours with the Brazil national team - lifting the Confederations Cup in 2013. He has more than 50 caps for his country, and has also regularly captained the side.

Kieran Tierney
Defender

Squad number: 3
Born: Douglas, Isle of Man, June 5, 1997
Joined Arsenal: from Celtic on
August 8, 2019

Scotland international defender Kieran joined us on transfer deadline day after a long association with boyhood club Celtic. The highly-rated left back came through the youth system at the Glasgow team, and soon gained hero status among the fanbase. He made his first-team debut aged just 17, and then won three PFA Young Player of the Year awards in succession north of the border. A tireless defender with a fearsome shot, Kieran is also able to play in central defence. He won four successive league titles with Celtic, as well as two Scottish Cups and two Scottish League Cups. He became a full international for Scotland in March 2016, aged just 18, and just a year later he captained his country during a friendly.

Nicolas Pepe
Forward
Squad number: 19
Born: Mantes-la-Jolie, France, May 29, 1995
Joined Arsenal: from Lille on August 1, 2019

Electrifying forward Nicolas became our record signing when he joined from Lille just before the start of the season. A left-footed winger who generally prefers to play on the right flank, the France-born Ivory Coast international can also play centrally, and had a superb goalscoring record last season. He netted 22 goals in the French top flight, and also contributed 11 assists – the only other player with at least 20 goals in 10 assists in Europe's top five leagues was Lionel Messi. Blessed with incredible speed, making him a dangerous weapon on the counter-attack, he is also a composed penalty taker. Usually known simply as Pepe, he won the Prix Marc-Vivien Foe in 2018/19, for best African player in Ligue 1, and played at the 2019 Africa Cup of Nations.

Gabriel Martinelli
Forward
Squad number: 35
Born: Guarulhos, Sao Paulo, Brazil, June 18, 2001
Joined Arsenal: from Ituano on July 2, 2019

A tricky winger with pace to burn, Gabriel was our first signing of the summer, arriving from Ituano of the Sao Paulo State Championship in Brazil. An excellent dribbler with a tremendous work-rate, the Brazilian teenager is most comfortable on the right wing, and is a wideman in the traditional sense, with great crossing ability. He was part of the squad on the pre-season tour to USA, and scored his first goal in the friendly win over Colorado Rapids in July 2019. Full name Gabriel Teodoro Martinelli Silva, he was called up to train with the senior Brazil national team ahead of the 2019 Copa America after a superb season with Ituano. He became his hometown club's youngest ever debutant, aged 16, in November 2017.

William Saliba
Defender
Squad number: TBC
Born: Bondy, France, March 24, 2001
Joined Arsenal: from St Etienne on July 2, 2019

Teenage central defender William was signed from St Etienne in the summer, and immediately loaned back to the Ligue 1 side for the duration of this season. Strong, powerful and excellent with the ball at his feet, he is regarded as one of the most promising young defenders in the whole of Europe. He made his St Etienne debut last season, aged just 17, and continued to impress throughout the campaign, making 19 appearances in all competitions. A powerful yet skilful right-footed defender, who is comfortable with the ball at his feet, he also uses his imposing 6ft 4in frame to great effect. He was coached by Kylian Mbappe's father while at hometown club AS Bondy, and has represented France at every youth level from under-16 to under-20.

HOW I MADE IT AT ARSENAL

BY AINSLEY MAITLAND-NILES

Our academy product tells us about his rise through the ranks at the Gunners, in his own words.

"Playing football is what you were born to do."

Those were my dad's words to me as I sat in the car, crying. I had just played the worst game of my life for Arsenal Under-13s.

"I don't want to play football anymore Dad, I'm finished," I'd told him. I'd said similar things to him before when I felt low after games for Arsenal, but this time was different. I meant it. I was going to stop.

As usual though my dad had some wise words for me, and by the time we had got home 20 minutes later, I had changed my mind.

In fact, I had changed everything. From that moment I changed my whole approach, the way I acted on the pitch and everything.

I know that if you want to get to the top, it's never a smooth ride. You have to make sacrifices. You have early nights instead of chilling with your schoolfriends because of training the next day. You can't always eat the food you feel like eating.

At the time you think you can have everything, do anything, but then you learn you need to balance it.

You have to push some things aside so you can focus, if that's what you really want to do in life.

And despite those low moments after some bad games for the academy sides, I knew this was what I really wanted to do.

My dad helped me see that, and so did my early coaches at Arsenal – Carl Laraman and Steve Leonard, who was a very good coach. Mark Arber as well – they all influenced me.

My brother, Cordi, also gave me a lot of advice. He's one of the reasons I got into football in the first place. He's two years older than me and my very first encounter with the sport was kicking around a ball on the sidelines when we went to watch him play at the weekend. That's when I knew I wanted to go into football. Well everyone wants to be like their older brother, right?

I was only four years old at the time, but a lot of my love for the game came from him. I used to train with him and his friends, until I joined Lakeview FC, who I played for every Sunday from the age of five.

By the time I was six I had been scouted by Arsenal and was now playing on Saturdays at the Hale End Academy.

A few scouts from different teams had been to watch me, but Arsenal was my local side, and it was the club that was always in my heart.

As a kid I used to watch quite a bit of football on TV with my dad; we always loved our sport growing up. I remember watching Bergkamp and Henry. I remember going to one game at Highbury, I think it was the last ever game there actually against Wigan, in 2006. I was about seven or eight years old.

I loved basketball as well as a kid, but now I was at Arsenal, so I had to choose a sport. And I chose to concentrate on being a striker.

That's how I started out, as a centre forward. I was fast and nippy, and loved getting behind the defences. My brother was a defender himself, at West Ham for a while, and he used to tell me what defenders hated playing against.

I scored quite a few goals up front. One of my favourite games at that time was away to MK Dons. I actually played in the number 10 role, and I loved it. I have fond memories of lots of games in the under-sevens and under-eights, but that one sticks out. I had a free role and I really enjoyed it, but what I really remember from that match is working hard and loving that side of it too. I think that game was the start of me picking up a work ethic, and really pushing on.

But when I was 12 I was told I was too small to be a striker, and they moved me to the wing.

I lacked motivation sometimes, and self-confidence, but my dad was always there to push me on.

So when I was 16, and got called to train with the first team one morning, he was the first person I told.

I was still a scholar, so you can imagine how nervous I was, joining in with all the stars at Arsenal back then. Neil Banfield came over to tell me to come with the first-team players. Neil was always pushing me to be the best player I could be, so I have a lot to thank him for, and for that first session especially. That day I remember he was always speaking to me, always on at me, always driving me forward, and it really helped.

It was nice to be close to some of the players as well – that first session was great. I must have done well because I got a smile from the boss, and you never got to see that much!

Afterwards I was delighted. I went straight to the changing room to text my dad "Dad, I just trained with the first team!" I was buzzing.

He was there by my side the following year, a couple of months after my 17th birthday, when I signed my first pro contract with the club. My mum and brother and agent were all there too.

I remember feeling so proud that I had achieved what I wanted – a professional contract. It was a wonderful feeling.

But I was also thinking, 'this is just a stepping stone. It doesn't mean anything, it's a reward for working hard, but what can you do next?'

Well a couple of months later I made my first-team debut. Arsène Wenger put me in the squad for the game away at Stoke on the Saturday. We went 3-0 down, brought it back to 3-2, but we had a man sent off so I never made it off the bench.

A couple of days later though I was travelling again, this time to Turkey for the Champions League game against Galatasaray. I thought I could get a game this time.

We had already qualified for the next round and so I was hopeful of playing. I spent the night before the game getting as much rest as I could. The next evening I was on the bench again. But at half-time I came on for Aaron Ramsey. We won 4-1 and wow, it was cool – making my debut away in the Champions League!

It is one of those moments that will never leave my mind. I still have the shirt, my mum got it framed and put up on the wall.

But my best memory of all came later. It was pre-season 2017, and I had just won the Under-20 World Cup with England in May, then travelled to Australia on tour with Arsenal in the summer. When we came back to England I was moved into the first-team dressing room permanently. That was the moment when I could look back on it all – all those training sessions, the sacrifices, the years in the academy – and say 'yeah, it was worth something.' I was where I always wanted to end up. All those years had been spent working towards that moment.

But I had changed a lot during that journey.

I was a really stroppy kid, I can admit that! As soon as something went wrong, I wouldn't be interested. But it changed as I grew up. Speaking to older people helped, trying to watch them and mimic them. Even watching the stars of the time, people like Thierry Henry – how they react and how they behave, it feeds into what you do as well.

I have changed everything, on the pitch and off it. As you get older you get more belief. Your passion for the game grows, and your ability increases as well as you work harder. You see those results, and it makes you keep pushing to get better and better every day.

Now as a player I have a lot of belief in my ability. I'm happy to play in a few different positions. Of course I have my favourite positions, but just as long as I'm in the team, I'm happy to do what I need to do when I'm on the pitch.

The one piece of advice that has stayed with me throughout my career so far though is that you get out what you put in from every day. If you don't work hard one day, that's the day you go missing. Every day is a chance to improve your knowledge of the game, your fitness and your technical ability, so make the most of it every day.

HIDDEN GUNNERS

Use your powers of investigation to work out which players are hiding here!

Answers on page 61

YOUNG GUNS

Arsenal's Under-18s won the Academy Premier League South last season. Here are three of the players who starred during the victorious campaign, and have already progressed to higher age groups.

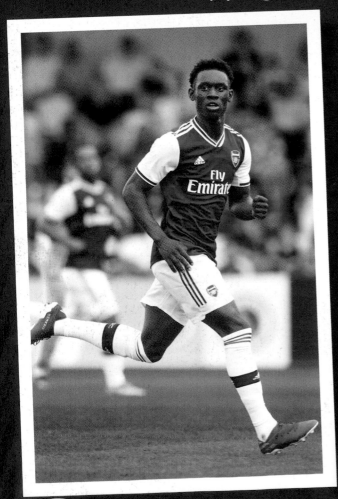

Folarin Balogun
Forward

Born: New York, USA, July 3, 2001

New York born forward Folarin was the top scorer in under-18 football for the whole country last season, racking up an incredible tally of 25 goals from 21 league games, as well as two more in the FA Youth Cup. The prolific front man is a natural goalscorer, as he has demonstrated since joining the club in 2012 at the age of 11. His tally last season included two hat-tricks and one four-goal haul – all achieved while still only 17. In fact, he averaged a goal every 62 minutes throughout the campaign, and was promoted to the under-23 side before the end of the season. He made five sub appearances at that level, scoring once, as well as appearing in the Checkatrade Trophy. It was no surprise that the club tied him down to a professional contract in February 2019 after showing stunning progression over the past couple of seasons – he also top scored for the under-18s in 2017/18. Now eligible to play for either England or USA in international football, he has already represented both nations at youth level. A right-footed striker who can also play just behind the front man, he added four assists to his 25 goals in the academy league last term.

Bukayo Saka
Forward

Born: London, September 5, 2001

Bukayo is a player already familiar to Arsenal fans after making a number of eye-catching cameos for the first team last season. Blessed with electric pace and a natural calmness in front of goal, the teenager is a constant threat from the left wing, and is rarely out of the action during a game. Last season he scored eight times from just six appearances at under-18 level – including two in the FA Youth Cup – but the majority of his football was played above his age group. He was a regular for Freddie Ljungberg's under-23 side in the Premier League 2, scoring five times, and was eventually rewarded by a call up to first team action by Unai Emery. He made his senior debut in the Europa League in November 2018, aged 17 and three months. That made him the 15th youngest player in the club's history - and he would also appear in the Premier League and FA Cup before the season was up. A product of the Hale End academy, Bukayo has grown up at Arsenal, progressing swiftly through the ranks and impressing the coaches at every level. An England youth international, the speedy winger – who has also played at full back – has represented his country at under-16, 17, 18 and 19 levels.

Arthur Okonkwo
Goalkeeper

Born: London, September 9, 2001

Towering goalkeeper Arthur enjoyed a breakthrough season at youth level, making his debut for the under-23s while still only 17 years of age. Tall and agile, he impressed for Freddie Ljungberg's side, playing four times throughout the season in the Premier League 2. He kept three clean sheets in those games, conceding just one in total. He was a valuable part of the under-18 league title-winning side as well. He played 10 times at that level, as well as twice in the FA Youth Cup. His progress didn't go unnoticed by the first-team coaching staff, and in March 2019 he was part of the squad that travelled to Dubai for some warm-weather training. There he spent the best part of a week working and learning alongside Petr Cech and Bernd Leno, impressing the coaches during training matches. Also eligible to represent Nigeria, Arthur is an England youth international, progressing to under-18 level last season. He has also worked his way through the ranks at Arsenal, since joining the Hale End academy, and has built up a reputation as a brave shot-stopper who is especially strong in one-on-one situations. Highly rated at the club, he signed his first pro contract shortly after turning 17 in 2018.

Bukayo Saka became the 15th youngest player in our history when he made his debut in November. He was **17 and 86 days.**

By avoiding relegation Arsenal confirmed 100 consecutive years of top-flight football – an English record!

We scored **112 goals** from our 58 matches, the 14th highest scoring season in our history.

STAT'S AMAZING!

Here are some weird and wonderful stats from season 2018/19

Xhaka covered the most ground in the Premier League (322.1 km), while **Aaron Ramsey** covered the most in any single game (12.7 km) v Manchester United in March.

Our undefeated run of 22 games between August and December 2018 was the joint-third longest unbeaten run in the club's history.

We picked up **five red cards,** for five different players.

Arsenal remained unbeaten through the month of November for the first time in 13 years.

Aubameyang and Lacazette contributed a combined 70 goals and assists in all competitions.

11 players made their Arsenal **debuts** in the season – five of them against Manchester City, five against Vorskla Poltava, and one against Blackpool.

Our only **hat-trick** of the season was scored by **Pierre-Emerick Aubameyang,** in the win at Valencia in the semi-final of the Europa League.

We kept 18 clean sheets in all competitions, and failed to score in seven games.

We scored at least twice in 11 successive matches between August and October – our longest such run since 1953.

We had 13 different kick-off times in the season – the most common was 8pm (13 games).

We were awarded **six penalties,** and scored **five** of them.

During the season Aubameyang scored at least once on every day of the week.

Granit Xhaka took the most touches of any Arsenal player in the Premier League **(2,784).**

Pierre-Emerick Aubameyang recorded the fastest speed of any Arsenal player – 34.75 km/h

We weren't leading at half-time in any of our first 17 Premier League games of the season.

Cumulatively we led matches for 36 hours and 38 minutes during the season, and we were behind for 15 hours and 37 minutes.

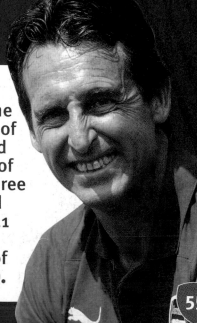

Unai Emery became Arsenal's 19th full-time manager – at the end of his first season he had already taken charge of more matches than three of the others, reached more cup finals than 11 of them, and had the best win percentage of them all **(60 per cent).**

In September we played **four home games within 10 days** for the first time in the club's history.

WORDSEARCH
FRENCH FANCIES

Can you find the 21 French players, in the grid below?

Answers on page 61

```
S A N O G O A D T H W S N R K
L P Y J Z N I E Q T V E B F O
K V R W G A W B A K M R G L S
M R P A B N I U K B N I X D C
K R S Y F K L C L J H P Y Y I
M C T X F Y T H E V M E H C E
D S Y Q N T O Y N T I C N N L
U Y A G M K R D A I I E Y R N
O V R L A X D M D L Q T I M Y
R K L V L N T N C T R R E R G
I D T L A A A N F T K G X P A
G L T S V M G C O Q U E L I N
K G R R I L G U E N D O U Z I
X I B R I N I M A L F R Q R T
Z W G N E T T E Z A C A L V H
```

Anelka	Gallas	Nasri
Clichy	Giroud	Petit
Coquelin	Grimandi	Pires
Cygan	Guendouzi	Sagna
Debuchy	Henry	Sanogo
Diaby	Koscielny	Vieira
Flamini	Lacazette	Wiltord

56

COMPETITION

Answer the following question correctly and you could win an Arsenal FC shirt signed by a first team player.

What was our most common scoreline last season?

A   1-0

B   2-0

C   2-1

Entry is by email only. Only one entry per contestant. Please enter AFC SHIRT followed by either A, B or C in the subject line of an email. In the body of the email, please include your full name, address, postcode, email address and phone number and send to: frontdesk@ grangecommunications.co.uk by Friday 27th March 2020.

UNAI EMERY'S FIRST SEASON

It was a ground-breaking season last term, as
Unai Emery became our first new manager for 22 years.
But how much do you remember about his debut campaign?

Who was the first player
to score a goal for us under
Emery?

How many games unbeaten
did Emery's team go between
August and December 2018?

Who was
named captain
most often
during Emery's
first season?

What was the
most common
scoreline in
Emery's first
season?

Who did Emery's first win as
Gunners boss come against?

Which player did Emery sign on
loan in January 2019?

Out of a maximum of 114 subs in
the Premier League last season,
how many did Emery make? 101,
107 or 113?

How many
players did Emery
hand a first-team
debut to in his
first season?

What is
the name of
Emery's Spanish
assistant coach
(pictured here)?

In which month did Emery win
every single game played?

TRUE OR FALSE?

Can you work out which of the following 12 statements are true, and which we have made up?

1. Matteo Guendouzi's brother is a jockey.

Alexandre Lacazette is Arsenal's top scoring number 9 in Premier League history.

3. Pierre-Emerick Aubameyang owns more than 30 cars.

Bernd Leno wears size six boots.

5.Nicolas Pepe owns a dog called Thierry.

Mesut Ozil gave up football for a year to concentrate on table tennis when he was younger.

7. Sokratis Papastathopoulos is fluent in seven languages.

David Luiz set a new world record when he joined Paris Saint-Germain in 2014.

9. Lucas Torreira's granddad once finished second in the Uruguay presidential elections.

Granit Xhaka used to be allergic to grass.

11. Rob Holding insists on having an even number for his squad number.

Hector Bellerin is a vegan.

vegan

Answers on page 61

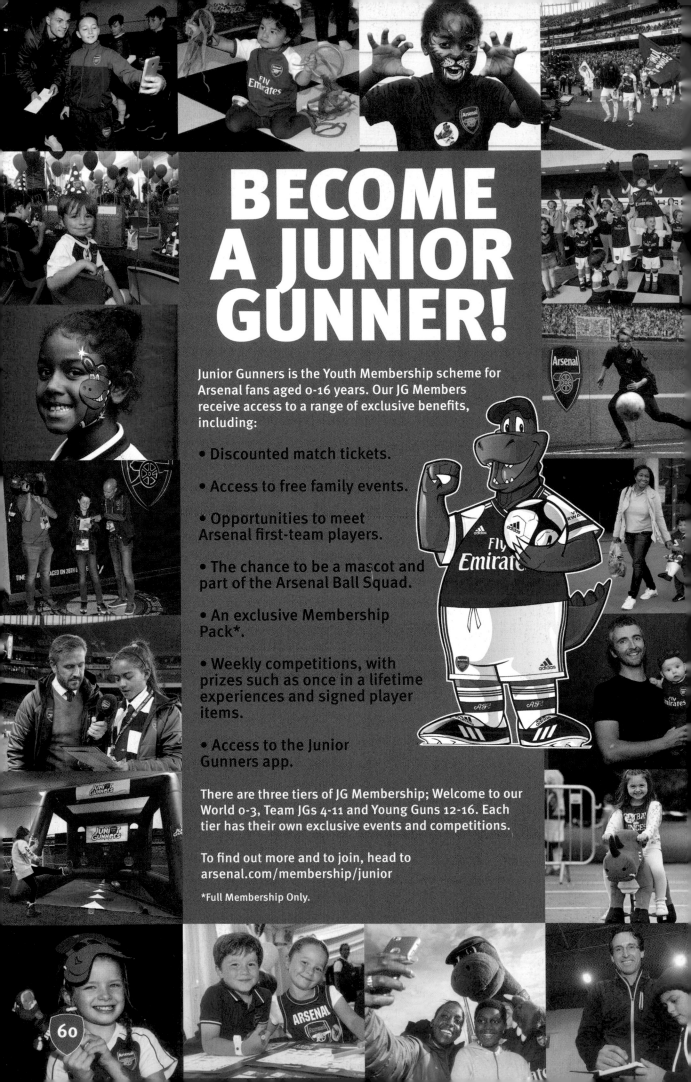

BECOME A JUNIOR GUNNER!

Junior Gunners is the Youth Membership scheme for Arsenal fans aged 0-16 years. Our JG Members receive access to a range of exclusive benefits, including:

• Discounted match tickets.

• Access to free family events.

• Opportunities to meet Arsenal first-team players.

• The chance to be a mascot and part of the Arsenal Ball Squad.

• An exclusive Membership Pack*.

• Weekly competitions, with prizes such as once in a lifetime experiences and signed player items.

• Access to the Junior Gunners app.

There are three tiers of JG Membership; Welcome to our World 0-3, Team JGs 4-11 and Young Guns 12-16. Each tier has their own exclusive events and competitions.

To find out more and to join, head to arsenal.com/membership/junior

*Full Membership Only.

60

QUIZ ANSWERS

Page 30 Spot the Difference

Page 31 Gaps in Your Knowledge

1. 5-1
2. Emirates Stadium
3. Aubameyang
4. FA Cup
5. Lacazette
6. Bournemouth
7. Premier League
8. 3-0
9. Stadio San Paolo
10. Valencia

Page 33 Who Scored More?

1. Nicklas Bendtner (47 to 41)
2. Andrey Arshavin (31 to 27)
3. Robert Pires (84 to 80)
4. Robin van Persie (132 to 120)
5. Aaron Ramsey (64 to 57)
6. Patrick Vieira (33 to 29)
7. Ray Parlour (32 to 28)
8. Lukas Podolski (31 to 20)
9. Olivier Giroud (105 to 99)
10. Gilberto (24 to 19)

Page 51 Hidden Gunners

1. Aubameyang
2. Maitland-Niles
3. Holding
4. Elneny
5. Lacazette
6. Mavropanos
7. Bellerin
8. Ceballos
9. Kolasinac
10. Mkhitaryan

Page 54 Wordsearch

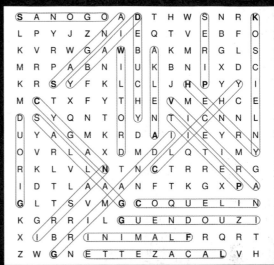

Page 58 Unai Emery's First Season

1. Henrikh Mkhitaryan
2. 22
3. Laurent Koscielny
4. 2-0
5. West Ham United
6. Denis Suarez
7. 113
8. 11
9. Juan Carlos Carcedo
10. September

Page 59 True or False?

1. True
2. True
3. False
4. True
5. False
6. True
7. False
8. True
9. False
10. False
11. False
12. True

SPOT GUNNERSAURUS!

WELCOME

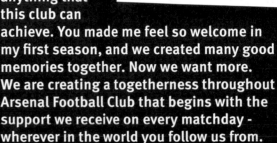

We are confident that this could be a very exciting season for Arsenal.

We began the process last season, my first year in London, and we have learnt a lot from that experience. The season did not finish how we wanted it to of course, but we can build on the promising elements within the team, and improve this year.

We have made many changes for this season - in the squad and off the pitch as well. You all know Freddie Ljungberg very well, and I'm delighted to have him working alongside me this season. Edu is another name that all Arsenal fans remember from the Invincibles team, and he had a busy first summer as director of football.

We also made some strong additions to the squad for this season, and we are all confident that we have a group of players who can achieve great things for the club - this season and in future as well. We are growing together, we are learning and we are building together - the staff, the players and, of course the fans.

I want to talk about the fans, because you are so vital to anything that this club can achieve. You made me feel so welcome in my first season, and we created many good memories together. Now we want more. We are creating a togetherness throughout Arsenal Football Club that begins with the support we receive on every matchday - wherever in the world you follow us from.

In return, I promise we will work every single day in training to be the best we can, and give everything we have every time the players pull on the Arsenal colours.

I have learnt a lot about what it means to be part of this club over the past 12 months – and I am now working hard every day to bring success here.

Unai Emery

ROLL OF HONOUR

League champions: 1931, 1933, 1934, 1935, 1938, 1948, 1953, 1971, 1989, 1991, 1998, 2002, 2004.
FA Cup winners: 1930, 1936, 1950, 1971, 1979, 1993, 1998, 2002, 2003, 2005, 2014, 2015, 2017.
League Cup winners: 1987, 1993.
European Fairs Cup winners: 1970.
European Cup Winners' Cup winners: 1994.
Charity/Community Shield winners: 1930, 1931, 1933, 1934, 1938, 1948, 1953, 1991 (shared), 1998, 1999, 2002, 2004, 2014, 2015, 2017.

2018/19

SEASON REVIEW